HANTS & DORSET A NATIONAL BUS COMPANY

Michael Hitchen

AMBERLEY

First published 2022

Amberley Publishing
The Hill, Stroud
Gloucestershire, GL5 4EP

www.amberley-books.com

Copyright © Michael Hitchen, 2022

ISBN 978 1 3981 0456 3 (print)
ISBN 978 1 3981 0457 0 (ebook)

British Library Cataloguing in Publication Data.
A catalogue record for this book is available from
the British Library.

Origination by Amberley Publishing.
Printed in the UK.

Introduction

Hants & Dorset as a National Bus Company was the amalgamation of two companies, Wilts & Dorset and Hants & Dorset. These two individual companies had alighted in 1964 when they were put under shared management. Both companies shared a similar history of ownership, being Tillings companies, and then became nationalised under the British Transport Commission. From 1969 both fleets carried Hants & Dorset legal ownership lettering; in September 1971 both fleets were numbered in a common scheme, and finally a full merger was made on 1 October 1972, after which only Hants & Dorset fleet names were applied to vehicles. This coincided with the introduction of the National Bus Company (NBC) corporate livery scheme, and NBC management decided that the red of Wilts & Dorset would be retained – albeit in the new poppy red shade. Buses would carry the new block lettering '**HANTS & DORSET**', with the new double N symbol. In 1970, the company had also assumed management of Gosport & Fareham, which carried the fleet name '**PROVINCIAL**'. Legal reason prevented a complete merger and Provincial would adopt the NBC green livery. Some service vehicles would carry the fleet names of Hants & Dorset as well.

On 5 September 1971, Hants & Dorset garages introduced colour-coded dots for allocation, based on three areas: Poole (Western); Southampton (Eastern); and Salisbury (Northern). The company had its central workshops in Southampton, on Shirley Road and Winchester Road (the bodyshop). These functions were moved in the late 1970s to Barton Park at Eastleigh. Its head office was at The Square, Bournemouth. Additionally, there were outstations and parking grounds at Alton (Alder Valley Garage); Baughurst; Bishops Waltham; Bowerchalke; Fordingbridge; Hindon; Hythe; Lyndhurst; Newbury (AV Garage); Petersfield (Southdown Garage); Porton Down; Romsey; Shaftesbury; Stockbridge; Warminster; Wimborne Minster; and Winterborne Kingston. Some of these, such as Hindon, had a building, but the majority were open parking areas. The following table shows the colour-coded allocation system:

Poole	White	Western Area main garage
Bournemouth	White and Black	Closed 29.11.80
Lymington	White and Orange	
Blandford	White and Grey	Outstation from 12.02.72
Ringwood	White and Pink	Outstation from 12.02.72.
Ringwood	White and Green	New code: Increased in size with Bournemouth closure

Swanage	White and Brown	
Southampton	Yellow	Eastern Area main garage
Fareham	Yellow and Black	
Winchester	Yellow and Orange	King Alfred Garage, retained until 1976
Woolston	Yellow and Pink	Closed 12.02.72
Salisbury	Blue	Northern Area main garage
Basingstoke	Blue and Black	
Andover	Blue and Orange	
Pewsey	Blue and Grey	
Amesbury	Blue and Pink	Outstation from 12.02.72

Hants & Dorset was quick to apply the corporate-style fleet name to vehicles, often on the existing livery irrespective of its shade of red or green, or the coach livery of the two former companies. It is interesting that they often used a shade of cream for the corporate lettering when applying on the existing liveries, which was more in keeping with the old shades. The NBC briefly allowed the use of cream lettering, but it was not part of the eventual corporate identity guidance, which specified 5-inch company names in white and, in Hants & Dorset's case, poppy red where applicable. NBC coaches were to be white with the company name in small black lettering underlined in the colour of the parent company (i.e. red). This scheme was soon modified to larger block lettering in red.

The combined fleet was one of the largest in the NBC (825 vehicles in 1975). The vehicles that formed the fleet in 1972 were largely influenced by its Tillings/BTC parentage, being mainly Bristol/ECW, but the fleet also contained a number of lightweight Bedford Coaches and Bedford buses with Willowbrook or Strachan bodies. The double-deck fleet were mainly 'Lodekkas', including rare Leyland engine FLF6Ls, and rear-entrance Bristol FL with unusual 30-foot-long bodies. The company's first rear-engine double-deckers were six Roe-bodied Daimler Fleetlines, originally intended for Gosport & Fareham in 1971. Both fleets contained Bristol MWs, with various ECW bodies, and Bristol REs with both bus and dual-purpose specification. The large fleet of Bristol LHs, of which the oldest was from 1969, were dual-door – a specification unique in the NBC to the Hants & Dorset/Wilts & Dorset.

The coach fleet at the time was an interesting mix of vehicles in either NBC white or the new red/white dual-purpose livery, though initially many coaches had corporate lettering applied to an existing mix of schemes, occasionally without the new logo. The early 1970s was a time of flux for the country; industrial issues forced bus companies to seek vehicles from other NBC constituents or non-standard types, with Leylands coming from Maidstone & District and Southdown, and oddments such as a single Bristol MW from Lincolnshire. The takeover of R. Chisnell & Sons Limited, better known as 'King Alfred', in April 1973 brought thirty-eight vehicles into the fleet. Many were non-standard types. Some only saw a brief service, while others lasted long enough to receive full NBC poppy red. In 1974, services and the garage at Swanage was transferred from Western National along with a small number of vehicles, including the only single-door Bristol RE with bus seating in use with Hants & Dorset.

Like most NBC fleets, the company took delivery of large numbers of Leyland Nationals and Bristol VRTs, though it continued taking Bristol LH/ECW and ECW-bodied Ford R1014s, which appeared at first glance the same as the more usual Bristol chassis versions. A small batch of five Ford R1014 buses were purchased again in 1976, though these had Plaxton Derwent bodies, a type rare in the NBC. These lightweight Fords were replaced in the late 1970s by an influx of Bristol LHs from Bristol Omnibus. The Market Analysis Project (MAP) of 1980 was made visible on vehicles with application of local identity names: 'Wintonline' for Winchester; 'South Wessex' for East Dorset; 'Antonbus' for Andover-based vehicles; 'Wiltsways' for South Wiltshire; 'Venture' for Basingstoke, a reference to the town's original bus operator; 'South Hants' for Southampton area services; and 'Provincial' for vehicles garaged at Fareham, reflecting the close cooperation with Gosport & Fareham that had developed under the NBC. This market-focused activity would not stop the biggest upheaval under NBC management when, under government direction to break up the larger NBC constituents, in April 1983 the company was divided into five new organisations. The Wilts & Dorset name returned along with Hampshire Bus for mainly stage services, and Shamrock & Rambler for coaching, though in 1984 Pilgrim Coaches was created for these operations around Southampton. Fareham services were transferred to Gosport & Fareham (Provincial) and central engineering activities at Barton Park, Eastleigh became H&D engineering/distribution.

The history of both Wilts & Dorset and Hants & Dorset is well documented elsewhere. Instead, this book is a pictorial study of the fleet operated in the 'double N' period. I remember owning *Fleetbook 11: Buses of South-East England* by A. M. Witton – in the 1970s these pocket-sized publications were often only form of reference for bus fleets, offering a fascinating insight into far away NBC fleets. Remembering this book, I often thought Hants & Dorset was one of the most varied in the NBC empire, made richer by the livery variations that were to be found. Hopefully the reader will appreciate the variety of the time. For completeness, I have included some vehicles that operated with the new companies after April 1983.

On 26 October 1986 the government deregulated the National Bus Company, in preparation for the ultimate aim to privatise all aspect of our state-owned bus company, once the largest in the world. Sadly, this was done for dogmatic reasons, and initial sales were often driven by property values. Services in the recently formed Hampshire bus area would go through a period of flux, especially around Southampton with Solent Blueline taking some services. Today services along the Solent south coast show no signs of their original operators, though the remaining Hampshire Bus area around Winchester, Andover and Basingstoke would become part of Stagecoach, which remains much the same today. Wilts & Dorset fared better; the operating area stayed much as before, and it would not have the indignity of the shabby operations with constant change that many former NBC constituents suffered in the late 1980s. The company stayed in local management ownership until recently, when it became part of Go-ahead South Coast, though sadly the Wilts & Dorset name is no longer applied to vehicles.

I must thank Peter Cook and John Weager for sharing their knowledge of the company, Pete Robinson for his assistance and insight into present day operations, and Graham Wareham, Alan Snatt, Mark Hampson, Dave Mant, David Flett, C. Richardsen and Steve Thoroughgood, for use of photographs. To all these individuals we must be thankful that they captured images in colour at a time when photography was not straightforward.

Like the majority of NBC companies, Hants & Dorset is now very much a memory, though it was once a common sight across a vast and diverse area from Basingstoke in the east all the way to Swanage and Blandford in the west. I hope the reader enjoys the following journey back to a simpler time, when poppy red buses could be seen in and around the busy city of Southampton, the picturesque New Forest, in the cathedral cities of Winchester and Salisbury, along promenades of the Dorset resort towns, through rural Hardy Country of East Dorset, across the lonely expanse of Salisbury Plain and out to the distant rolling Wiltshire Downs.

9 (131 ANW), 60 (SLJ 757H), 17 (HAM 502E), Andover Garage, 1973

Three Hants & Dorset coaches stand inside Andover Garage, all with corporate fleet names applied to their pre-NBC livery. Nearest is Bristol MW/ECW 9 (131 ANW); next is 60 (SLJ 757H), a Bedford VAL; furthest is 17 (HAM 502E), a Bedford VAM. Both Bedfords have Duple Northern bodywork. All had come from Wilts & Dorset, and all have blue/orange garage codes for Andover.

17 (HAM 502E), Bournemouth Bus Station

Bedford VAM 17 is seen again, still allocated to Andover, but had since received corporate NBC dual-purpose livery, which had been applied in November 1973. All this batch were disposed of in 1976. 17 (HAM 502E) was subsequently owned by Carreglefn Coaches on Anglesey. One of this batch received green NBC local coach livery while transferred to Provincial. (Mark Hampson)

53 (LMR 733F), Salisbury Garage, 28 March 1975

51–54 (LMR731–734F), new to Wilts & Dorset in 1968, were Bedford VAL70s fitted with Duple Northern bodywork. 53 is seen at its home garage in 1975. Hants & Dorset had a number of these lightweight 'Chinese Six' coaches for touring work. As much of its area covered traditional holiday locations, they were ideal. (Dave Mant)

57/58 (PEL905–906G), Salisbury Garage, 10 June 1978

In 1969 Wilts & Dorset purchase another four Bedford VAL70s, again with Duple Northern bodywork. As can be seen, Duple had restyled the bodywork. Nos 57 and 58 both display the blue dot code for Salisbury Garage. Both these two would be withdrawn in 1978. (Dave Mant)

63 (WEL 803J), Southampton Garage, 13 April 1979

Another Bedford that came from Wilts & Dorset, 63 is seen at its home garage in 1979. Unlike the similar earlier vehicles, 63 is in full NBC NATIONAL white livery. The double steering was unusual type in the NBC; apart from Southern Vectis, and some in the central activities groups such National South West, this configuration was rare in the NBC bus operating fleets. (Dave Mant)

109 (684 AAM), Southampton Garage

109 was a Bristol FS6G with ECW H33/27RD bodywork. When the two fleets were amalgamated, former Wilts & Dorset vehicles were numbered in the 1–999 series, and vehicles from the original Hants & Dorset were allocated in the 1000–1999 series.

170 (TTF 220M), Eastleigh Garage, 1984

In the early 1980s it was a common sight to see coach-bodied vehicles downgraded to dual-purpose liveries throughout the NBC. Such a vehicle was Hampshire Bus 170, a Leyland Leopard with Duple C49F bodywork. It was ex-National Travel (West) 120, one of four numbered 170–173 (NT West 120/191/192/133) that came south in 1984. Alongside is Leyland National 3708 (UFX 851S), a native from Hants & Dorset.

174 (XBW 74M), Southampton Garage, 1984

Another second-hand, dual-purpose, coach-bodied vehicle transferred to Hampshire Bus was 174, a Bristol RELH6L that was new in 1973 to City of Oxford (as 74). Apart from these two second-hand batches (see 170 in the previous image) and five ex-Shamrock & Rambler coaches, the fleet was made up of bus-bodied Bristol REs, Bristol VRTs, Leyland Nationals and a few Bristol LHs.

607 (MMW 355G), Trowbridge Bus Station

Dual-purpose Bristol RE 607 carries the 'Wiltsway' local marketing identity used for vehicles allocated to the South Wiltshire garages. The 241 Salisbury–Trowbridge (via Warminster) service was a joint working between Hants & Dorset and Bristol Omnibus.

613 (RLJ 799H), Andover Bus Station

Andover's Bristol RE 613, with forty-five-seat dual-door bodywork, waits to work the 276 service to Basingstoke. The town's bus garage can be glimpsed in the background. Today Andover does have a purpose-built bus station on a new site, but the garage, like many others, is a simple facility on an industrial estate.

632 (CRU 142L), Southampton Garage

Wilts & Dorset bought thirty-two Bristol REs between 1969 and 1972, including eight finished as dual-purpose. Dual-door Bristol RE 632 was the last in this batch and passed into the Hampshire Bus fleet when Hants & Dorset was divided in 1984.

692 (JKK 203E), Basingstoke Garage, 1974

Both the Wilts & Dorset and Hants & Dorset companies received Willowbrook-bodied Leyland Panthers from Maidstone & District in 1971/2. 692 was in the Wilts & Dorset batch of seventeen numbered 684–699 (M&D 3095–3110). After working from Tadley, 692 is seen at Basingstoke bus station with the garage visible in the background.

696 (JKK 207E), Southampton Bus Station, 1974

Another former Maidstone & District Willowbrook-bodied Leyland Panther that came via Wilts & Dorset, locally allocated 696, is seen departing the town's bus station in West Marlands Terrace, opposite the civic centre. This location is now a shopping centre.

751 (JAM 418), Basingstoke Garage, 7 September 1974

Still showing traces of its former Wilts & Dorset ownership, Bristol LS, 751 of Salisbury garage, stands (possibly out of use) at Basingstoke Garage. Hants & Dorset keenly applied NBC corporate fleet names on the pre-1972 liveries. (Steve Throughgood)

807 (SWV 688), Basingstoke Garage, 1973

Wilts & Dorset still had thirty-two Bristol MWs in 1972 when the fleet was merged with Hants & Dorset. They carried a number of ECW bodywork styles. The roof lights on 807 show it had started life as a coach; by the time it was seen here, it had been fully declassified to a bus.

815, Bournemouth Bus Station, 25 March 1974

New the same year as 810, seen above, Bristol MW, 815 was finished by ECW with another variation of coach bodywork. 815 stands in the ill-fated Bournemouth bus station, awaiting return to its home town on the X38 limited stop service.

834 (EMT 299D), Andover Garage, 21 June 1975

New to Wilts & Dorset in 1966, Bristol MW 299 was fitted with dual-purpose seating, but using the ECW body more associated with a bus. Note the additional chrome trim often fitted when designated as dual-purpose. (Steve Throughgood)

820 (XMR 950), Basingstoke Bus Station, 1974

Basingstoke, though in Hampshire, was formerly in Wilts & Dorset operating area, with a garage in the town. Locally allocated Bristol MW 820 started service as Wilts & Dorset 803 in 1961 at Salisbury Garage, was repainted in NBC poppy red livery as late as June 1974 and sold in September of the same year.

857 (HEL 391D), Winchester Bus Station, 1973

857 was a later Bristol MW, new in 1966 it was one of the last surviving Bristol MW in the fleet being withdrawn in 1976. It would see further use with Silcox in West Wales.

1015 (FEL 750D), Beulieu, 16 April 1975

New in 1966 as Hants & Dorset 903, Bristol MW 1015 of Southampton Garage looks smart newly painted in NBC dual-purpose livery in February 1974. The lack of any destination blind would have limited it use on stage services.

1017 (FEL 752D), Bath Road, Bournemouth, 1973

In the same batch as 1015 above, 1017 is seen turning off St Peter roundabout, heading towards the seafront and looking superb in freshly painted NBC dual-purpose livery. It was used mainly on tours and excursions from the south coast holiday resort. The white and black of Bournemouth Garage are not obvious when applied on a white base.

1022 Salisbury Coach Station, 24 May 1975

Poole Garage's 1022 is seen on National Express service 757 from Bournemouth to Cheltenham. Though in suitable livery for this work, 1022, from the same batch as 1017 above, was painted in full NATIONAL white livery. 1022 would be loaned to Gosport & Fareham in 1977 before withdrawal in May 1978. (Dave Mant)

1024 (JEL 423E)

1024 had the unusual combination of Bristol RESH with a Duple C40F body. New in 1967 with only thirty-two seats, it was reseated to forty in 1974. It would also carry NBC dual-purpose livery before withdrawal in 1981.

1052 (AEL 7B), Bournemouth Bus Station, 1975

Hants & Dorset only purchased two Bristol REs with classic C47F coach bodywork. 1051/2 were new in 1964; strangely neither were fitted with destination blinds. Instead the illuminated 'Holiday Tours' panels were fitted. Hants & Dorset never painted these in NATIONAL white livery. Unfortunately, both perished in the Bournemouth bus station fire in July 1976. (Mark Hampson)

1055 (MRU 127F), Southampton Garage

Another corporate NBC fleet name on a non-standard livery, 1055 was fitted with the striking Duple Northern Commander III bodywork, slightly unusual is the combination with the Bristol RELH chassis. Part of a batch of three (1053–55), they were all withdrawn in 1978. (Mark Hampson)

1056 (ORU 579G), Swanage, 31 August 1973

Still in pre-NBC livery, 1056 was new as Hants & Dorset 921 in 1969, part of a batch of three numbered 921–923 (ORU 579–581G), renumbered in 1971 to 1056/1093/4. Only 1056 was retained by Hants & Dorset; the other two were transferred to Shamrock & Rambler (496/7) in August 1973.

1057 (REL 741H), Bournemouth Bus Station, 1975

1057 (former 924) was in a pair purchased in 1969. These would be the last Bristol RELH coaches for the company. Fitted with Duple Northern 'Commander IV' bodywork, they were used mainly on extended tour work.

1059 (SRU 999H), Bournemouth, 1980

Basingstoke's 1059 was new in 1970 as a single purchase. Originally numbered 934, it was a Leyland Leopard with Plaxton Panorama Elite C40F bodywork. Hants & Dorset painted it in NATIONAL white in 1973 while allocated to Southampton Garage. By 1980 it had been downgraded, and was allocated to Basingstoke, carrying 'Londonlink' vinyls, similar to Alder Valley services into the capital. It was sold in 1981 and found new use with Ashtree Coaches of Edenfield (Lancs).

1061 (WEL 464J), Basingstoke Garage

Another of Basingstoke's dual-purpose coaches was 1061. Note how the Plaxton bodywork had been restyled when compared with 1059, seen in the previous image. When new this vehicle had forty seats, reseated to forty-nine in 1976. Conversion to dual-purpose came in 1979. It was withdrawn in 1983.

1153 (ALJ 573B), Southampton Garage, 10 June 1978

Locally allocated, 1153 was a Bristol Lodekka FS6G, new to Hants & Dorset in 1964 as 1500. Hants & Dorset had a large fleet of rear entrance Lodekkas, with sixty-two still in service in 1976. Withdrawal came in 1979.

1210 (7685 LJ), Canford Bottom, 1974

An unusual Bristol FL6G, 1210 works the lengthy 22 Bournemouth–Wimborne Minster–Corfe Mullen service. Hants & Dorset Lodekkas were fitted with a metal sun visor above the driver windscreen. 1210 would finish its time allocated to Ringwood outstation. It lasted a little longer than others in the batch, being withdrawn in 1980.

1242 (GRU 976D), Poole Bus Station, mid-1970s

Bristol FLF6G 1242 pulls out of Poole bus station, which was receiving a coat of paint at the time. This bus station remains open today, as does the nearby garage – both dating from the early 1970s.

1250 (HRU 678E) and 2303 (HOR 591E), Poole Garage, 18 April 1975

Bristol FLF6G, 1250, was one of the later Lodekkas bought by Hants & Dorset. Allocated to Bournemouth Garage, it is seen with similar allocated 2303, a Leyland Atlantean/Roe H74F. 2303 was one of four that were taken over from King Alfred in 1973.

1258 (KRU 235F), Southampton Bus Station, 20 September 1975

Several NBC constituents painted double-deck vehicles in London and Manchester Assurance all-over advertising livery, with an attractive carnation flower logo. This vehicle had moved between Winchester, Southampton and finally Poole garages. 1258 was a Bristol FLF6B.

1379 (KRU 982), Poole Bus Station, June 1973

The Bristol KSW survived long enough to received NBC corporate fleet names in only a handful NBC constituents. Hants & Dorset 1379 was new in 1952 (as 1316). It would last until 1974 before withdrawal. Bristol Omnibus was the last company to operate the KSW in normal service. (David Flett)

1392 (LRU 58), Southampton Bus Station

Another late survivor, Bristol KSW 1392 (former 1329) is still in pre-corporate green livery but with corporate fleet names. Hants & Dorset applied these in cream for use on the pre-1972 liveries.

1419 (RLJ 505), Fareham Garage, January 1974

Seen outside Hants & Dorset Fareham Garage, Southampton's 1419, a 1955 Bristol LD6G, again displays cream fleet names on original green livery. This practice was unusual but not unique to Hants & Dorset. Fitted with the deep radiator typical of early Lodekkas, 1419 (former 1355) was withdrawn in 1975. (Graham Wareham)

1464 (UEL 721), Southampton Garage, 1973

Though the NBC had decided that Hants & Dorset would be a poppy red fleet, its not obvious in this view. 1464 was allocated to Eastleigh Garage's (yellow and grey dots) when seen in the early 1970s. A Bristol LD6G, formerly 1400, was new in 1958. It would last until 1976, though it was probably not painted into NBC poppy red.

1503 (JLJ 52E), Swanage Former Railway Station Site, 25 August 1973

Hants & Dorset purchased a number of Bedford VAMs with B33D Stratchen bodywork in 1967, a very unusual purchase for a former BTC company. None received NBC livery, though 1504 (former 827) did receive a corporate fleet name.

1505 (JRU 459E), Bournemouth Bus Station

The single purchase of its type in 1967, 1505 had the same chassis as 1504 seen in the previous image, though was finished with Willowbrook B33D bodywork. Note the cut-away front for working on the Sandbanks Ferry. (Mark Hampson)

1506 (MRU 64F), Salisbury Garage

In 1968 the company took delivery of a further ten Bedford VAMs with Willowbrook bodies. Bournemouth Garage's 1506 is seen standing over in the yard of Salisbury Garage after working into the city from the South Coast. (Mark Hampson)

1509 (MRU 67F), Bournemouth Bus Station, 19 August 1974

One of this batch, 1509, was rebuilt in June 1970 after accident damage. It received a new front and lost its centre door; it was also the only one to receive NBC poppy red livery. It is seen between Bristol RE 1649 and similar Bedford VAM 1509, both still in Wilts & Dorset livery. 1509 was withdrawn in February 1975 but did see further use with Moore of Windsor.

1528 (REL 792H), Fareham Garage

Seen outside its home garage, Bristol LH, 1528 shows the unusual dual-door body fitted to the seven new to the company in 1969. Both companies had favoured small buses fitted with dual doors, including ECW-bodied Bristol MWs.

1538 (ULJ 368J), Southampton Garage

Hants & Dorset received twenty-eight Bristol LHs between 1969 and 1972, including ten with the unusual door bodywork. These were followed by seven with single-door bodywork, still with the early flat front but with dual lights. The 'South Hants' local identity was applied to vehicles used in the Southampton area.

1545 (XEL 831K), Salisbury Garage, 14 June 1975

As with the Bristol RE, the Bristol LH received a restyled front in 1971; 1545 show this feature when seen in 1975, still in original green livery. It would receive NBC poppy red and was used from Southampton Garage. After withdrawal it would be sold to Castlepoint Bus Company in Benfleet (Essex). (Steve Throughgood)

1623 (RLJ 342H), Poole Garage

Between 1969 and 1972 Hants & Dorset purchased forty-nine Bristol RELL6Gs. Fifteen were dual-purpose and the remainder were all forty-four-seat-dual-door buses. 1623 at Poole Garage was from the early flat-fronted batch.

1624 (TRU 216J), Poole Garage, June 1982

Later Bristol RE deliveries, both bus and dual-purpose, were fitted with the restyled curved front design. 1624 stands in Poole Garage, with its locally allocated South Wessex identity vinyls. The dual-door arrangement is clearly visible. Hants & Dorset only had one single-door bus-seated Bristol RE, 1652 (LDV 459F), which had come from Western National with the transfer of Swanage Garage in 1974.

1643 (UEL 563J), Southampton Bus Station, 1973

Still carrying the dual-purpose livery Hants & Dorset applied to the ten Bristol RELL6G delivered in 1972, just before the corporate livery was introduced, though it carries a corporate fleet name. Later this batch would later be painted in local-coach red and white livery.

1647 (XLJ 722K), Bournemouth Bus Station, 1973

Another dual-purpose Bristol RE in pre-NBC livery, 1647 is seen on the upper level of Bournemouth bus station.

1647 (XLJ 722K), Bournemouth Town Centre, May 1975

Looking superb, recently painted in NBC local coach livery. Dual-purpose Bristol RE 1647, new in 1972, was one of the last vehicles to be delivered to Hants & Dorset before the two fleets were fully amalgamated.

1652 (LDV 459F), Swanage Bus Station, 1974

1652 was Hants & Dorset's solitary single-door bus-seated version of the Bristol RE. Formerly with Western National until 1974, when the services and the garage at Swanage were transferred to Hants & Dorset. Seen outside the former railway station, before the preservation society returned rail services to the town, which was in use as the Hants & Dorset bus station.

1685 (DKE 265C), Eastleigh Garage

Both Wilts & Dorset and Hants & Dorset purchased second-hand Leyland Panthers with Willowbrook bodies from Maidstone & District in 1971/2, buying seventeen and sixteen vehicles respectively. They initially operated in various liveries some with corporate fleet names applied. Formerly Maidstone & District 3040, 1685 is seen in the mid-1970s, by which time it was in the correct poppy red livery.

1789 (SRU 979), Salisbury Bus Station

Bristol LS 1789 was new as 803 in 1956. Interestingly it was delivered as a dual-door bus, an unusual combination on this chassis/body. It was converted in November 1958 to single-door. By the time it was seen in the early 1970s, still in Hants & Dorset green, the type was becoming rare in NBC use.

1803 (XEL 553), Salisbury Garage, 5 October 1974

1803 was a Bristol MW bus new in December 1958 (811). It lasted long enough to receive NBC red in September 1974. Seen soon after repaint at its home garage, it was withdrawn in January 1975. (Dave Mant)

1810 (YEL 229), Basingstoke Bus Station, 1973

At the time the two fleets were combined in 1972, and the corporate livery was introduced, the fleet still contained numerous variations of Bristol MW types and livery combinations. New in 1959, 1810 was a Bristol MW, originally a thirty-seat coach (870). It was converted to a bus in February 1967; at least two of this type (1806/7) were painted in poppy red in 1974.

1827 (1473LJ), Southampton Bus Station, 1973

Another vehicle in pre-NBC livery carrying corporate fleet names, 1827 was new as coach 881 to Hants & Dorset in June 1961 and downgraded in 1969 to dual-purpose OMO. It would last until February 1975 before being sold for scrap.

1831 (7121LJ), Winchester Bus Station, 1973

Bristol MW 1831 (new in 1962 as 885) was one of the last Bristol MW in the Hants & Dorset fleet, surviving into 1977. It received NBC poppy red bus livery in March 1974 and retained coach seats until withdrawal.

1832 (7122 LJ), Southampton Bus Station, April 1975

1832 was a Bristol MW coach from 1962 (886), downgraded to dual-purpose in September 1969. In March 1973 it was painted into the 'Seaspeed' livery for dedicated service to the Southampton hovercraft terminal. It was withdrawn in April 1976.

1833 (7123 LJ), Southampton Docks

In March 1973 another Bristol MW was painted in a special dedicated livery, in this case for the Red Funnel crossings to Cowes. This service ran from Southampton railway station and the Royal Pier. 1833 was repainted in NBC poppy red bus livery in September 1975, but was withdrawn in August 1976.

1905 (VRU 128J)

In 1971 Hants & Dorset took delivery of its first rear-engine double-deckers, six Daimler Fleetlines with Roe bodywork. They had been diverted from Gosport & Fareham in exchange for a similar number of undelivered Bristol REs.

1906 (VRU 129J)

Yet to receive NBC corporate red livery, 1906 displays the classic advert for the National Bus – 'together we're going places'. Another of the six Daimler Fleetlines, 1906, still carries it original green livery, but with cream corporate fleet names. An unusual type for the fleet, they lasted into the new Wilts & Dorset fleet in 1983.

1906 (VRU 129J), Poole Garage

1906 is seen again but has since been painted in NBC poppy red livery. Note the Hants & Dorset Leyland Sherpa van 9055, new in April 1978.

1908 (OJD 197R), Bournemouth Town Centre, mid-1980s

In 1982 and 1983 Hants & Dorset purchased thirty former London Transport DMS, Daimler Fleetline/ Metro-Cammells. All were converted to single-door before entering service. A number carried Hants & Dorset fleet names, but photographs are rare. Twenty passed to the new Wilts & Dorset and ten to Hampshire Bus. They made an unusual sight outside the capital; here 1908 (Poole Garage) loads in Bournemouth with a service to Poole.

1926 (OJD 245R), Southampton Garage

Hants & Dorset/Hampshire Bus received ten of the former LT DMS buses in 1983. 1926 was DMS2245 when in London Transport use; it would be painted in Hampshire Buses' red, white and blue livery after privatisation, and would see further use with Fareway in Liverpool.

2003 (PFX 744R), Swanage Bus Station

An unusual purchase in 1976 was three Alexander-bodied Ford A0609 (a fourth went to Provincial). They were allocated to Lymington (2001), Blandford (2002), and Swanage (2003). Unfortunately, they gained a reputation for unreliability, Minibuses were a very rare item in NBC fleets in the 1970s. Except for these three minibuses, the 2xxx number series was used generally for vehicles taken over from other fleets.

2008 (JHO702E), Winchester Chesil Station, April 1974

At first glance this appears to be a usual NBC type of coach, but in 2008 was taken over from R. Chisnell & Sons, better known as King Alfred of Winchester. Hants & Dorset took over their operations on 29 April 1973, along with thirty-seven vehicles. In common with other NBC constituents that absorbed independents in the 1970s, the takeover brought a number of interesting non-standard types into the fleet. 2008 was loaned for a short time to Gosport & Fareham. (Mark Hampson)

2009 (BCG 701J), Wembley, 8 March 1980

Hants & Dorset numbered all the former King Alfred vehicles in the 2xxx series. 2009 was a Bedford YRQ with a Duple C45F body, and was the only former King Alfred coach to receive central activities group white livery. (Alan Snatt)

2044 (ROW 565G), Salisbury Garage, 4 August 1973

Recently repainted in NBC local coach livery, 2044 was a Ford Transit with twelve-seat South Hants bodywork. The company received seven similar vehicles with the King Alfred takeover. A very unusual vehicle for a National Bus Company, they had a complex history of transfer to the service fleet and some back into PSV use. 2044 became service vehicle 9053 in August 1975 for use at Basingstoke Garage. (Dave Mant)

2051 (CCG 704C), Salisbury Garage, 17 August 1974

A similar type to existing Hants & Dorset coaches, ex-King Alfred 2051 looks superb recently repainted in local coach livery. A Bedford VAL14/Plaxton C49F, it was new in 1966. Allocated to Southampton Garage, it survives today preserved in King Alfred green livery. This garage location in Salisbury remains open today, a rare survivor in the deregulated era. (Dave Mant)

2052 (EOU 703D), Winchester Garage, April 1974

The other Bedford VAL taken over form King Alfred was 2052, seen still in its original livery, but with NBC fleet name applied. 2052 was repainted in local coach livery the same as 2051 in the previous image. In 1976 this vehicle was transferred to Gosport & Provincial, receiving Provincial fleet names on green/white local coach livery.

2201 (WCG 106), Winchester, September 1973

2201 stands in Winchester garage yard soon after takeover. Hants & Dorset wasted no time in applying its
fleet numbers to the ex-King Alfred vehicles. Four rear-entrance AEC 'Bridgemaster' (2201–4) came with the
takeover. 2203 was cannibalised for spares and 2204 was used for a short time, being withdrawn in 1973. 2201
and 2202 were both withdrawn in 1975; neither received NBC red livery.

2211 (595 LCG), Winchester, September 1974

The other AEC double-deckers brought into the fleet with King Alfred's operations were 2211/2, a pair of AEC Renowns with front entrance Park Royal bodies. Both received full NBC livery. 2211 was withdrawn in 1976, while 2212 lasted into the following year.

2303 (HOR 591E), Winchester Garage, August 1974

The only other double-deck vehicle to come from King Alfred were four modern Leyland Atlanteans with Roe bodywork. Numbered 2301–4 (HOR589–592E), they were used from both Winchester and Poole garages. The four vehicles passed to Bristol Omnibus in 1979, becoming Bristol 8600–03. Bristol converted three (2301/2/4) to open-top for use at Weston-super-Mare and Bath. 2304 (HOR 592E) is preserved in its original livery, with the roof from 2303.

2602 (AOU 109J), Harestock, May 1973

Three Metro-Scanias with MCW bodies were briefly taken into stock from King Alfred. 2601–3 (AOU 108–110J) were new in 1971; Hants & Dorset applied numbers and depot codes only. By October 1973 they had been exchanged them with London Country for three Leyland Nationals. London Country renumbered them to MS5–7. LCBS already had this type in use and painted them in yellow/blue Superbus livery for local services in Stevenage. Not a successful design, they were withdrawn in 1977. (David Flett)

2651 (412 FOR), Winchester Chesil Station, 1974

Three ex-King Alfred Leyland Leopard/Willowbrook B53Fs were new in 1962. They became 2651–3. 2652 was painted in NBC red in June 1973, and is seen soon after standing in the former King Alfred yard, which Hants & Dorset retained for a few years after the takeover. (Mark Hampson)

2653 (414 FOR), the Broadway, Winchester, 1973

The last of the three, 2653, stands near the King Alfred statue on the Broadway in Winchester. It had used a similar departure stage in its former ownership. All three were painted into NBC poppy red in summer 1973; oddly the company applied its fleet name on the lower sides on all three vehicles, occasionally using the roof for advertising. All three were withdrawn in 1977.

2697 (UOU 417H), the Broadway, Winchester 1973

Another three Leyland Leopards (2697–9) came from King Alfred. They had Plaxton Derwent B52F bodies. Never a common type in the NBC, especially in the southern region, all three received NBC poppy red. 2697 had fleet names applied on the bodysides, while 2699 carried them on the roof panel. They lasted until 1979. All three found further use in South Wales with Morris (2697/8), Creamline (2697/8) and Rees & Williams (2699). (David Flett)

2697 (UOU 417H), the Broadway, Winchester 1973

King Alfred certainly brought a wealth of interesting non-standard vehicles into the fleet in 1973. 2697 is seen again now in NBC red livery. Two of the three survive in preservation (2697/9), both in their former green livery – though 2697 was preserved in NBC red for a time.

2702 (SCG 856), the Broadway, Winchester, 24 November 1973

More unusual ex-King Alfred vehicles were the five Leyland Tiger Cubs with Weymann bodywork. WCG 855 and WCG 856 became 2701 and 2702 and had Weymann dual-purpose bodywork. Hants & Dorset painted both of them in NBC red bus livery. Both saw further service; 2701 in Scotland and 2702 with Eynon of Trimsaran in South Wales. (David Flett)

2703 (WCG 103), Winchester, 30 December 1973

The other three Leyland Tiger Cubs, 2703–5, also had Weymann bodywork, though fitted with bus seats. 2703/4 received NBC red livery, though all were withdrawn in 1974. (Dave Mant)

2704 (WCG 104)

Sold by Hants & Dorset, 2704 is seen still carrying its fleet number while in use with Eynon of Trimsaran in South Wales. WCG 104 is another King Alfred vehicle that survives in preservation.

3001 (FJA 225D), Southampton Garage, 7 April 1973

Hants & Dorset used numbers above 3000 for vehicles taken into stock after the 1972 amalgamation. An interesting second-hand intake in 1973 were five Leyland Leopards with Duple Commander C41F bodies, which had come from North Western RCC (225–229). North Western had recently been divided between Crosville, Trent and SELNEC. Seen in an interim livery with NBC fleet names but no logo, 3001 was withdrawn in 1977, the last of the batch going the year after. Note the former Maidstone & District Atlanteans in the background. (Dave Mant)

3005 (FJA 229D), Cheltenham Coach Station, 28 August 1976

3005, another of the ex-NWRCC Leylands, is seen in NBC local coach livery – again devoid of any logo. 3002/3 carried this same livery. After sale, 3005 would be used by Sergeants of Wrinehill in North Staffordshire, near the Cheshire border. (Alan Snatt)

3004 (PUF 267M), Salisbury Garage, 5 December 1981

The company reused the fleet numbers 3001–3005 again in 1980 for another second-hand transfer. They were a batch of Ford R1114/Duple C49F new to Southdown (1406/10/21/27/30) in 1974. They only saw brief use with Hants & Dorset, the last going in 1982. (Dave Mant)

3010 (SJA 411K), Poole Garage, 29 November 1981

Yet another ex-North Western RCC vehicle (411), SJA 411K had gone to National Travel (West) (N81) when North Western was broken up. 3010 came south in 1981 but would only see a year service with the company. (Dave Mant)

3055 (ORU 383M), Salisbury Garage, 28 February 1981

3055 was new to Hants & Dorset in 1974, a Leyland Leopard with a Plaxton Panorama Elite III C44F body. Five, 3051–5, were purchased and given NBC central activities group white livery. Two of the batch (3051/2) were destroyed in the Bournemouth bus station fire of 1976. 3055 was sold in 1986 to a private operator, Donnelly's Coaches in Eire. (Dave Mant)

3056 (NEL 111P)

Brand new 3056, a 1976 Leyland Leopard/Plaxton C49F National white coach, is seen while being delivered to Hants & Dorset. One of five, it had not yet received its fleet number or depot code, which would be Bournemouth, when new. This batch was transferred to Shamrock & Rambler in April 1983, though two soon moved to the new formed Pilgrim Coaches. NEL 111P would move on to Midland Red West (441) in November 1984, painted in the Midland Express red and yellow livery, and then on to Western National and later a number of independents.

46 (3061) (SRU 146R), Lower Maudlin Street, Bristol, June 1984

The company took delivery of another four Plaxton Supreme-bodied Leylands in 1977: 3061–4 (SRU146–9R). 3061 had become 46 in the Shamrock & Rambler fleet when caught departing Bristol Marlborough Street bus station with the National Express 786 service to Portsmouth.

3065 (WPR 501S)

3065/6 of 1977 carried familiar restyled Duple bodywork but had Bedford YMT chassis. Both were short lived with the company being sold in 1980. WPR 501S found use with operators in Gatwick and back in Southampton with Roger's.

3070 (ELJ 208V), Salisbury Bus Station, 4 October 1979

Hants & Dorset bought four new coaches in 1979, all Leyland Leopards with Plaxton Supreme IV C53F bodywork. Plaxton Supreme IV had a restyled front giving a different appearance. All four were transferred to Shamrock & Rambler in April 1983. Interestingly 3070 passed back to Hampshire Bus, the Stagecoach company. (Dave Mant)

3075 (RUF 806H), Eastleigh Workshops, 24 May 1981

In 1981 Hants & Dorset took a large number of second-hand coaches into stock. 3075 Leyland/Duple Commander IV was new to Southdown in 1970 as 1806. The batch of eleven (3074–85) lasted only to the following year, but 3075 continued in NBC use with Shamrock & Rambler. Amazingly, the chassis from 3075 was exported to Australia, where it received a new body in 1984. (Dave Mant)

3082 (HCD 381E), Southampton Garage, 29 October 1977

Another former Southdown coach, 3082 was part of a batch of three (3080–2) Leyland Leopard/Duple C49F new in 1967 as Southdown 1779–1781 and transferred in 1977. Again, the company only retained these vehicles for a year, or two in the case of 3082. (Dave Mant)

3084 (ARN 792C), Salisbury Garage, 7 April 1977

Other second-hand coaches taken into stock in 1977 included six Leyland/Plaxton Panorame Elite C49F (3083–8). All were new to Ribble MS between 1965 and 1967. Again, they only enjoyed a short life with Hants & Dorset – all were gone by 1979. (Dave Mant)

3092 (161 AUF), Marwell Zoo

In 1973 Hants & Dorset took delivery of five ex-Southdown Leyland Leopards fitted with the rare Weymann Castilian bodywork. A design that was unique to Southdown, the five were numbered 3091–4 by Hants & Dorset, all receiving NBC red and white dual-purpose livery. 3092 is seen on an excursion to Marwell Zoo near Winchester. The striking, if dated, design can be appreciated in this view.

3097 (AJA 147B), Gloucester Green Bus Station, Oxford

Another unusual second-hand purchase was five Leyland Leopards with the stylish Alexander Y-type bodywork. AJA 145–49B were new to North Western RCC in 1964 (145–9) before passing to National Travel (North West) and becoming N145–9 in 1973. The rest of this batch went to Crosville and Trent, who also painted them in local coach livery. Salisbury's 3097 is seen on excursion work at Oxford in the mid-1970s.

3098 (AJA 148B), Basingstoke Garage, July 1978

3098 was allocated to Basingstoke, seen here parked in the yard of its home garage. Fitted with coach seating, they were occasionally pressed into National Express use. All the company's Y-types had been withdrawn by 1977.

3304 (CRU 304L), Basingstoke Bus Station, 1974

Delivered in 1972/3, 3301–6 (originally numbered 1301–6) were the first Bristol VRTs to enter service with the company. They were also the first new vehicles delivered in NBC poppy red livery with white band and grey wheels. Hants & Dorset never operated the flat-fronted version of the ECW-bodied Bristol VRT.

3323 (JJT 435N), Southampton Garage, August 1975

Hants & Dorset only took delivery of Bristol VRTs from 1972, so only operated versions with the series 2 curved front panel, or later. 3323 stands inside the large garage at Bedford Place in Southampton. Note a very rare glimpse of an Austin JU250 service van in the background. (Graham Wareham)

3345 (NEL 115P), Salisbury Bus Station, 23 April 1983

When the fleet was divided, 3345 went to the newly formed Hampshire Bus Company. The fleet name appears to have been applied in a somewhat non-standard fashion! 3345 waits to depart from Salisbury back to Andover, its home garage; this service still operates today jointly between Go-Ahead South Coast and Stagecoach South. (Dave Mant)

3347 (NEL 117P), Southsea, 13 June 1976

Hants & Dorset was a user of the Bristol VRT in the rare dual-purpose variation. Very few NBC constituents acquired this version. Ideally suited for inter-urban routes between the Solent conurbation, 3347 is seen on display at Southsea in summer 1976.

3373 (RPR 719R), Southampton Garage, June 1979

Hants & Dorset in the 1980s applied several all-over adverts to its Bristol VRTs. 3373 received adverts for the Carrefour hypermarket, a brand better known in France. It was repainted in October 1979, still for Carrefour but in white livery.

3374 (UFX 855S), Poole Garage

Bristol VRT 3374 of Poole Garage (white dot). Seen when new, careful observation reveals its detachable top. Six with this feature were delivered in 1977; they were all transferred in 1979 to Southern Vectis in exchange for 671–6 (UDL671–6S), which gained H&D numbers 3414–9.

3390/1 (VPR 489/90S), Southampton Garage, 1984

Two consecutively numbered Bristol VRTs, 3390/1, stand in the rain outside Southampton Garage. Both had passed to Hampshire Bus when the company was divided in 1983. Both later received Hampshire Bus red, white and blue livery.

3404 (BFX 572T), Poole Garage, June 1981

Bristol VRT 3404 carried advertising for 'Mr Drinks', which extended all around the vehicle between the decks. 3404 would later receive similar sized adverts for Triangle Computers and all-over advertising for Sherry & Haycock, a building supplier. Note the 'South Wessex' local identity fleet names, introduced to vehicles operating from Poole Garage in 1981.

3415 (UDL 672S), Poole Bus Station, Summer 1979

One of the six Bristol VRTs exchanged with Southern Vectis, 3415 (ex-SVOC 672) is seen still in NBC green livery. All six were allocated to Poole Garage, replacing the same number of convertible open-top versions that were made surplus due to service revision with the local council.

3431 (GEL 681V), Salisbury Bus Station, 9 December 1982

3431 looks incongruous in snow while standing in Salisbury bus station in winter 1982. Sadly this location no longer exists, having been redeveloped; buses now depart from stands on the roadside, scattered across the city. (Dave Mant)

3446 (KRU 846W), Southampton Garage, 1984

Hants & Dorset would operate 150 Bristol VRTs in the years up to 1983. 3446, new in 1981, was in the last batch of eleven to be purchased (3445–56) and was painted in all-over advertising for Allegro Computers in 1984. It had passed to Hampshire Bus by the time its was seen here. In 1988 it would be sold to United Counties.

3475 (975 CWL), Southampton Garage, 11 September 1975

3475, a 1958 AEC Regent V/Park Royal, was new to City of Oxford (975) but had come from Gosport & Fareham (Provincial) in 1975. A sole example, it was very short lived and unpopular with staff, lasting only a few months before it was sold into preservation. (Graham Wareham)

3477 (VAP 33), Marlborough High Street, November 1975

Working the 205 from Swindon to Salisbury, a service still operating today as Salisbury Red's X5, 3477 was a Bristol FSF. Note the shorter body when compare with a Bristol FLF. VAP 33 was new to Southdown in 1961 (2633). (Dave Flett)

3477 (VAP 33), Salisbury Garage, 29 November 1975

Pewsey's allocated 3477 is seen at Salisbury Garage. One of six purchased from Southdown in 1974/75, 3477 was sold for scrap in April 1977. (Dave Mant)

3482 (OPN 801), Bournemouth, 1976

Another former Southdown Bristol Lodekka, 3482 was a Bristol LDS6B, new in 1959. Three came to Hants & Dorset in 1976, 3482–4, all open-top versions. They only lasted into 1977. This series of numbers had been used previously for second-hand Bristol Lodekkas. (Dave Mant)

3486 (75 JNO), Salisbury Garage, 24 September 1975

In June 1974 Hants & Dorset purchased six second-hand Bristol LD5G Lodekkas from Eastern National. Still in ENOC green, which would have been similar shade to Wilts & Dorset pre-1973 livery. Note the centre band has been painted white and the company has applied the corporate fleet name in cream, but the logo is white. Two of the six were destroyed by fire at Basingstoke in 1974. The rest, including 3486, had all been withdrawn by January 1976.

3505 (DEL 541L), Winchester Garage, June 1975

Hants & Dorset purchased seventy-nine Bristol LH6L with ECW B43F bodies between 1973 and 1975. Both constituent companies had taken delivery of the flat-fronted Mark 1 version between 1969 and 1972, including some unique dual-door versions. 3505 was an early delivery in 1973 and was withdrawn in 1980.

3537 (ORU 537N), Sandbanks Ferry, March 1975

The Sandbanks Chain Ferry linking Sandbanks (Poole) to the Isle of Purbeck had limited clearances when driving off the ramp. The company modified vehicles by cutting away the lower front, as seen here on 3537 working to Swanage. Previously Bedford VAMs, such as 1506 featured earlier, were similarly modified. Note the letter 'F' below the fleet number to indicate this modification.

3539 (ORU 539N), Shell Bay, 28 August 1974

On the Isle of Purbeck, with Poole and the Isle of Wight in the background. Another Bristol LH with cut-away bodywork for the chain ferry, 3539 prepares to return to Swanage in the summer of 1974.

3570 (HJT 42N), Andover Bus Station, February 1982

Ready to work service 281 to Hurstbourne Tarrant, towards the northern extremes of the company's operating area – a standard Bristol LH, 3570 of Andover Garage, carrying the local Antonbus fleet names carried by vehicles from this garage, named after the river that runs through the town.

3585 (RRU 585N), Salisbury Garage, 14 September 1974

Brand new 3585 stands in the yard of Salisbury garage in 1974. Sharp-eyed observers will notice this is not a Bristol LH, but a Ford R1014. An unusual combination for an NBC constituent, possibly purchased because of supply difficulties at the time. Identifying features including the wheels are not inset, and the headlights sit proud of the front bodywork. (Dave Mant)

3597 (RRU 597N), Upavon, 14 June 1975

Another Ford R1014, 3597 of Pewsey Garage stands in the turning bay outside the Antelope Inn in Upavon, a village on the northern edge of Salisbury Plain. This vehicle was in a batch of twenty-five from 1974, part of two sequences – 3580–99 and 3801–5. All were allocated to South Wiltshire Garages. (Steve Throughgood)

3619 (NEL 862M), Bournemouth Bus Station, 23 August 1974

On a service more suited to a coach-seated vehicle, though Hants & Dorset had yet to receive the dual-purpose bus-version Leyland National. 3619 is seen while still new. It was delivered in unrelieved poppy red and with original white double N logos and fitted with the large roof pod, which Leyland changed to a shorter version on deliveries from later in 1974.

3625 (NPD 108L), Southampton Bus Station, 30 December 1973

The 'PD' registration indicates a vehicle not issued locally. NPD 108L started life with London Country as their LN8, arriving at Hants & Dorset along with two others in exchange for the ex-King Alfred Metro-Scanias, 2601–3 (AOU 108–110J) new in 1971. London Country already operated a small number of Metro-Scanias, so was probably instructed by the NBC to take them in exchange for nearly new Leyland Nationals.

3628 (SEL 236N), Lymington Garage, 1980

3628 stands in the yard of Lymington Garage, which is located alongside the town's railway station. Hants & Dorset operated 151 Leyland Nationals, including three dual-door types from LCBS. All the Leyland National new to company were single-door versions, in both 10.3 and 11.3 m versions. Twenty were dual-purpose versions.

3629 (SEL 237N), Southampton City Centre, 1984

New in 1974, by 1984 3629 was in the Hampshire Bus fleet. Here it awaits departure from Southampton on a Calmore Estate (Totton) local service. Sadly, the newly formed company discontinued the coloured depot-allocation dots.

3634 (GFX 973N), Winchester, 27 August 1976

Hants & Dorset operated twelve short (10.3 m) Leyland Nationals. 3634 was in the first batch, 3633–7 of 1974. They seated forty-one, unlike the long version that seated forty-nine. (Alan Snatt)

3643 (GLJ 679N), Bristol City Centre, June 1984

Hants & Dorset took its first dual-purpose Leyland Nationals in 1975, numbered 3638–47 (GLJ674–683N). In 1983 one went to Provincial (3638) two (3639/47) passed to Hampshire Bus and the remainder (3640–46) to Wilts & Dorset. A number were dedicated to the X41 limited stop service between Salisbury and Bath/Bristol. 3643 nears its journey end in the summer of 1984.

3644 (GLJ 680N), Warminster, May 1984

Wilts & Dorset 3644 stands over at Warminster while working the X41 to Bath. This service still operates today as the X4 (First Group).

3723 (TEL 489R), Andover Bus Station, March 1982

3723 was the first in the second batch of dual-purpose Leyland Nationals. Another ten were delivered in 1977/8, numbered 3723–32. After April 1983 they became 3723–25/29/31/33–35 with Hampshire Bus; 3726-27/3730 with Wilts & Dorset; and 3728/32 with Provincial Bus. Vehicles being moved according to their garage allocation, as apposed to grouping vehicle together by numbers.

3727 (TEL 493R), Bournemouth Triangle Bus Station

After the disastrous fire that destroyed Bournemouth's split-level bus station in July 1976, services were hastily transferred to the Triangle. The original bus station was not rebuilt and services continued to use this less than ideal location. Here, 3727 in Wilts & Dorset service awaits departure for Southampton on a X2 limited stop service.

3742 (DRU 7T), Southampton Bus Station, Summer 1980

One of the last Leyland Nationals to be delivered to the company, 3742 was new in 1979 in a batch of four. The following year saw the Hants & Dorset take delivery of 3745–51. Hants & Dorset did not operate either Leyland National Series B or Mark 2 versions.

3814 (NJT 831P), Blue Boar Row, Salisbury, July 1980

The company took another delivery of Ford R1014 lightweight buses in 1976, this time with Plaxton Derwent bodywork. Only five were purchased (3812–3816), and all were allocated to Salisbury Garage. They were a rare type in the NBC; Maidstone & District, East Kent and Midland Red also operated them. 3814 waits in Blue Boar Row, a stand for a number of local services that did not use Salisbury bus station.

3826 (REU 332S), Southampton Garage, 1981

The Ford R1014 were withdrawn in the early 1980s and replaced by a number of second-hand Bristol LHs from Bristol Omnibus. In total forty-one were obtained in 1981. 3826 was previously Bristol 421. This vehicle would pass to Solent Blue Line in November 1987 and Trimdown Motor Service in June 1989.

3837 (WAE 294T), Poole Garage, 18 April 1982

Complete with Hants & Dorset fleet name, 3837 retains it NBC green livery from Bristol Omnibus. (Dave Mant)

3899 (RFE 461), Bournemouth Bus Station, 1973

3899 was new to Lincolnshire Road Car Company (2818) in March 1961. It was acquired by Hants & Dorset in June 1973 for use on the contact service between Bournemouth and the Atomic Energy Establishment at Winfrith. It was repainted in poppy red bus livery with a white band in December 1974 and renumbered as 829. It stayed in service until December 1976 before being sold to Martins in Middlewich, who sold it on for further use in the North West and latterly Eire.

3904 (A904 JPR), London Victoria Coach Station, 1986

Prior to privatisation, the reformed Wilts & Dorset chose this scheme for its dual-purpose vehicles. 3904 arrives at Victoria, completing the 88-mile journey from Salisbury.

3905 (A905 JPR), Salisbury Coach Park, August 1984

After the companies was divided in 1983, both Wilts & Dorset and Hampshire Bus purchased Leyland Olympians with ECW bodies, a type that Hants & Dorset did not operate. Wilts & Dorset purchased five (3901–5) all fitted out dual-purpose and painted in correct corporate NBC livery. 3905 was allocated to Pewsey Garage (blue/grey dot), for use on the number 5 Salisbury–Swindon service.

3995 (528 HKJ), Poole Garage, 16 March 1975

1973 saw five 1960 Leyland Atlanteans transferred from Maidstone & District. The company numbered them 3995–9, the highest numbers used by Hants & Dorset for PSVs. 3995 was M&D 5528 and all had Metro-Cammell bodies. They lasted until 1976, when they were transferred again, this time to Western National. 3995 became WNOC 976. (Dave Mant)

3028 (TFH 161R), Bournemouth, Late 1980s

Formerly National Travel South West 161, 3028 was an AEC Reliance with Duple Dominant 2 C55F bodywork. It operated briefly with the Shamrock & Rambler fleet name. The route 700 was the Western Venturer, a long-distance Penzance–Plymouth–Exeter–London service.

3033 (WFH 165S), Bristol, 1983

Shamrock & Rambler retained its identity in 1973, becoming part of the NBC central activities group as part of National Travel South West. Already closely associated with Hants & Dorset, in 1981 its operations were transferred to Hants & Dorset. In the 1983 division of Hants & Dorset it would become its own company. New in 1978, Leyland Leopard 3033 was National Travel (SW) 165 until 1981. It only operated in the new Shamrock & Rambler company until early 1984, when it moved to Hampshire Bus.

3017 (PDG 112M), London Victoria Coach Station

Seen in the orange and blue livery adopted by Shamrock & Rambler in 1984, 3017 had been Black & White 112 when new in April 1974. Movement within the National Travel South West constituent fleets were complicated – this vehicle moved to Shamrock & Rambler in 1981, and would eventually be sold to Poole Scout Band and re-registered 128 EKJ.

3099 (BPR 99Y), Marlborough, May 1985

Painted in the NBC venetian blind livery that was used across the NBC in the mid-1980s, Shamrock & Rambler 3099 (which later carried the name *Falcon*) was a Leyland Tiger with Duple Laser bodywork (Dominant V). New in 1983, it was subsequently used by both London & Country and Midland Fox.

9051 (LOR 666F), Bournemouth Triangle, 18 August 1979

Photographs of NBC commercial service vehicles – vans or lorries – are very rare. Hants & Dorset converted a number of the former King Alfred minibuses for service use. 9051 of Poole Garage was formerly bus 2041. Converted to a van in 1975, it was withdrawn in 1981.

9052 (AFH 529T), Swanage Bus Station, Late 1970s

Hants & Dorset used Ford, BMC (Leyland) and Bedford commercial vehicles during the NBC era. The white livery and NATIONAL lettering is as directed by the NBC corporate livery manual. Bedford CF pick-up 9052 was new in September 1978 and allocated to Holdenhurst Road, Bournemouth. It is seen outside the former railway station, which serves as the town's bus station. At this time the railway preservation society was still re-laying track on the former trackbed. (C. Richardsen)

9077 (ORU 532M) and 3435 (GEL 685V), Salisbury Garage

Bristol LH 9077 was converted in February 1983 from bus 3532, an unusual conversion as a former double-deck vehicle was normally the starting point for a tree cutter. Seen alongside Bristol VRT 3435, which still carries a towbar from a recent recovery, 9077 only carried Wilts & Dorset fleet names.

9081 (t/p 141 MR), Weymouth, 1973

Bristol L5G bus 729 (BOW 162) was extensively rebuilt by Hants & Dorset as a heavy recovery lorry 2006. In 1955, it originally had a crane. It was moved from Southampton Garage to Salisbury in exchange for the AEC Matador heavy recovery vehicle 9084. 9081 would be withdrawn in November 1977.

9082 (BOW 169)

9082 was Bristol L5G towing conversion of 1956 (former bus 504). The company converted three Bristol L5G for recovery. 9082 retained its original cab and bonnet; the other two conversions (9081/3) were complete rebuilds. 9082 was allocated to Basingstoke until replaced by an ex-Green Goddess Bedford RL 9085. 9082 still exists in preservation.

9082 (6228 EL), Southampton Bus Station, March 1976

Bristol MW towing vehicle 9082 was converted in October 1975 for use at Southampton Garage. Originally bus 1819 (875 when new), it was repainted in NBC red in 1974 while still serving as a PSV. It was replaced in 1978 by the Bristol LH 9079.

9083 (ERU 513), Poole Garage, 24 August 1974

9083 show the extensive bodywork conversion on the Bristol L5G chassis. Rebuilt in 1959 from bus 729, it became Hants & Dorset 2022 in the service fleet, renumbered 9083 in 1971. It was withdrawn in 1981. Today it is preserved.

9087 (NLJ 528M), Poole Garage, August 1981

Bristol LH 9087 (ex-3528) replaced 9083, seen in the previous image, and was converted in August 1981. It carried trade plates 282 EL. Poole gained a Ford D recovery lorry (9081) soon after the company was divided in 1983.

9088 (REL 745H), Salisbury Garage

Bristol LH bus 1524 was converted to a publicity vehicle in April 1978, possibly for use in the MAP work around the time. It would be repainted from time to time according to the promotion. 9088 passed to Hampshire Bus in 1983.

9091 (HHR 62), Andover Garage, June 1975

Hants & Dorset reused its 90xx service fleet numbers. An earlier version of 9091 was this Bristol KSW Trainer converted in April 1968 from bus 335. Allocated to Salisbury Garage, it would be withdrawn in April 1977.

9091 (DKE 264C), Poole Garage, April 1983

9091 stands in Poole Garage yard in 1983. A Leyland Panther one-person-operation training vehicle, 9091 was converted in June 1978 from bus 1684. This was one of the ex-Maidstone & District Panthers acquired in 1972.

9092 (OHR 919), Eastleigh Workshops

Hants & Dorset would retain its trainers for about five years. Here a Bristol LD (ex-bus 428) stands in the yard of the Central Workshop in Eastleigh. It was converted in September 1976 for use at Poole Garage and was withdrawn in May 1981.

9093 (5678 EL), Southampton Garage, 8 June 1979

Salisbury-allocated 9093 stands in the yard of Southampton Garage in 1979. Converted in April 1978 from bus 1116, it was withdrawn in June 1982.

9095 (SRU 971), Salisbury Garage

Hants & Dorset had specialist training vehicles for conducting training. 9095 was a Bristol LS bus 857, converted to this role in October 1972. It would last until December 1977, probably the last Bristol LS vehicles (with a coach body) in NBC use.

9204 (EMR 294D), Poole Garage, 13 September 1987
Hants & Dorset's last half-cab driver trainers were five Bristol FLF6G numbered 9201/3–6. Originally Wilts & Dorset bus 678 (later H&D 213), 9204 was converted in 1983 and shows traces of it previous fleet name when seen in Poole Garage yard in 1987.

Amesbury Garage, 27 May 1986
Amesbury Garage (blue/pink dot) had closed as long ago as 12 February 1972, after which it served as an outstation of Salisbury. The depot ceased use of the building sometime later, with buses parked in the bus station area. Today the area is a car park and supermarket.

Andover Garage, 5 August 1984

Andover Garage (blue/orange dot) had a large garage positioned beyond the bus station. With an allocation of twenty-nine vehicles in 1982, the garage survived into the late 1980s before moving to an industrial estate outside town. The bus station fared a little better, being rebuilt on a nearby site.

Basingstoke Garage Yard, April 1974

Basingstoke Garage (blue/black dot) was alongside the bus station. The company's most northerly garage, it had fifty-two vehicles allocated in 1982. Oddly Basingstoke was originally part of the Wilts & Dorset company, but passed to Hampshire Bus in 1983. Today the entire area is unrecognisable under a large shopping development.

Basingstoke Garage Yard, April 1974

This view gives an idea of the variety that existed in the Hants & Dorset fleet in the 1970s. The garage was visible from a car park access ramp, so like Poole was well photographed.

Blandford Garage, 4 August 1984

Blandford Garage (white/grey dot) in Salisbury Road is seen in the ownership of the reformed Wilts & Dorset company. It had an allocation of fourteen vehicles. The building survives today as a supermarket.

Shamrock & Rambler Garage, Holdenhurst Road, Bournemouth

Shamrock & Rambler's garage in Holdenhurst Road, Bournemouth was also the headquarters of the company. After the fire at Bournemouth bus station in 1976, this garage was used to assist Hants & Dorset in the town. Eventually the company would move vehicles to Ringwood and Poole, leaving this as the only NBC garage in the town.

Blenheim Road Yard, Eastleigh

Eastleigh Garage was originally in Blenheim Road, which was closed in 1978 – after which Barton Park became the location for the garage and central works, when the company closed its two sites in Shirley Road Workshop and Winchester Road Bodyshop, Southampton. These new premises used buildings that were formerly British Railways carriage and wagon workshops. The garage was adjacent to the main workshops. The site remains in bus use with Blue Star.

Fareham Garage, 1975

Hants & Dorset had a garage in Fareham. At this time the area had its own NBC constituent in Gosport & Fareham, which carried Provincial fleet names. With the split of Hants & Dorset in 1983 this garage was closed and vehicles transferred to Provincial at their nearby Hoeford Garage.

Fordingbridge Outstation, October 1974

3004 (FJA 228D) is seen in the Fordingbridge car park, used as an outstation of Salisbury Garage. Later vehicles were stabled in the grounds of the comprehensive school in Downton. In the 1970s, the NBC used open sites like this all across the country to overnight vehicles.

Hindon Garage, 2 August 1984

Hindon was another outstation of Salisbury. A simple corrugated building, it could house two vehicles inside with a couple in the yard to the left at the rear of a public house.

Lymington Garage, 3 August 1984

Lymington Garage was near the town railway station. It had an allocation of fifteen vehicles; the bus station was situated nearby in the town. This garage is still in bus use with Go-Ahead South Coast.

Pewsey Yard, September 1975

Pewsey Garage (thirteen vehicles) was a number of sheds that could only accommodate single-deck vehicles. Sighted near local council offices in Frog Meadow, the site lasted into the privatised era, in recent years moving to an industrial unit just outside of town.

1014 (FEL 426D), Poole Garage, June 1974

Poole Garage is located under the multistorey car park that serves the town's shopping centre and bus station. One of the company's largest allocation with seventy-seven vehicles, it had moved from a location in the town in the early 1970s. With the division of the company in 1983, in the absence of a central workshops this garage assumed that role for Wilts & Dorset. Today it remains open with Go-Ahead South Coast.

9082 and 1152, Poole Garage, mid-1970s

A well-known vantage point for the Poole garage yard and passing Southern Region Weymouth line is the multistorey car park built over the garage. Recovery tender 9082 was a long-term resident of Poole garage, alongside Bristol FS6B 1152.

Poole Garage Yard

Poole garage yard is seen again with visiting Alder Valley Leyland National 137; Salisbury's Bedford coach 62; Bournemouth's Lodekka 1250; and locally allocated Bristol RE 1639.

1905, Poole Garage, mid-1970s

One of the six Roe-bodied Daimler Fleetlines, new in 1971, stands outside the garage at Poole. The unusual location under the multistorey car park is clear.

1912, Poole Garage Yard

The ex-London Transport DMS Leyland Fleetlines were bought by Hants & Dorset in 1982/3. 1912 stands at Poole along with Bristol LHs 3856 and 3852, Bristol RE 1624, and a Leyland National still with the original white logo. It isn't clear, but the Fleetline may carry the Hants & Dorset fleet names that this type carried briefly.

Ringwood Garage, 3 March 1974

1501 (HRU 695E) of Bournemouth (white/black dot) is seen in the yard of Ringwood garage. The garage became on outstation in 1972 but returned to garage status with the closure of Bournemouth garage.

Ringwood Garage, 21 May 1989

Ringwood garage is seen in the reformed Wilts & Dorset days. The small garage building is visible behind Leyland National 3750 (FPR 66V). The garage passed to Wilts & Dorset in 1983 and remains operational today in Go-Ahead South Coast ownership. (Dave Mant)

Salisbury Garage, 2 August 1984

Salisbury's Castle Street Garage is an unusual survivor. The site east of Castle Road remains open, much as it did in NBC days – though originally it had buildings both sides of the road and served as Wilts & Dorset central workshops as well. With an allocation of eighty-four vehicles in 1982, only Southampton had a larger allocation.

Salisbury Garage, 7 June 1986

Another view in the Wilts & Dorset era – note the Ford Transit service van. Amazingly this garage remains much the same today, conveniently located and now under Go-Ahead ownership.

Southampton Garage, 27 May 1986

Southampton Grosvenor Square Garage was the company's largest with an allocation of ninety-one vehicles. The site adjoined the city's coach station; the bus station was the other side of the guildhall in West Marlands. All the Southampton premises were sold off soon after privatisation, the depot became housing and offices. The bus station is now the Marlands shopping centre, leaving the city with no bus station to this day.

Winchester Road Bodyshop, Southampton

A rare view inside the Bodyshop in Winchester Road, the central workshops were located in Shirley Road, both locations were replaced by the Eastleigh Barton Park Workshops, and both sites redeveloped. The company also retained a former tram depot in Parkstone (near Poole) as a repair facility until the early 1970s.

Winchester Garage, April 1973

Two of the recently taken over King Alfred buses are inspected by staff in their new environment. Winchester Garage was positioned with the city's bus station, in the Broadway. Buses had to drive through the building to enter the bus station. It had an allocation of thirty-one vehicles in 1982. The company retained the former King Alfred Garage in Chesil Street until 1976, after which it was used for storage and workshops, closing in 1980. The main garage building was demolished in 2018, though the bus station was retained. Until 1980 Winchester also had a dedicated coach station in Worthy Lane. The company also had garage buildings in Bournemouth, Swanage and Ringwood. Ringwood Garage in West Street is still open, while the Swanage Garage building is still standing, though buses are now parked in the open near the railway station. Bournemouth Garage was under the town's bus station but was destroyed by fire in 1976. (Mark Hampson)

Fleet No:	Reg No:	Make and Type	Chassis Type	First Lic'd	Body	Allocated to
9050	PBW 18M	Guy B.J.4.T.	JT20138 / Flat Bed Trailer (8050)	1/74 (8050)	Tractor Unit and Tanker (7050)	CBW
9051						
9052	APW 529T	Bedford Lorry	9736087626091	9/78	Pick Up Van	Holdenhurst Road Bournemouth
9053	AOD 407T	Leyland Marina	49927M	11/78	Van	Poole
9054						
9055	JAA 133S	Leyland Sherpa	ZCPABJ/051371N	4/78	Van	Salisbury
9056	JHO 31S	Leyland Sherpa	ZCHABK/052033N	6/78	Pick Up	CBW (Stores)
9058	JAA 132S	Leyland Sherpa	ZCPABJ/051370N	4/78	Van	Salisbury
9059						
9060	HAA 216P	Bedford CF	ET609275	8/75	Pick up Van	Grosvenor Square
9061	HAA 815S	Leyland 850	XKV1/519291A	4/78	Mini Van	Salisbury Traffic Inspectors
9062	HAA 812S	Leyland 850	XKV1/478230H	3/78	Mini Van	Basingstoke Traffic Inspectors
9063						
9064	HAA 814S	Leyland 850	XKv1/194888A	3/78	Mini Van	Southampton Traffic Inspectors
9065	BRU 190T	Austin Morris 850	XKV1/572651A	3/79	Mini Van	Poole Traffic Inspectors
9066	XPX 73V	Leyland Sherpa 250	ZHPPL56N/91366	9/79	Van	Poole
9067	XPX 76V	Leyland Sherpa "	ZHPPL18N/91360	9/79	Van	Salisbury
9068	XRV 551V	Leyland Sherpa "	ZHPPL18N/93359	10/79	Van	CBW
9069	KOM 811P	Ford Escort 1100	BBAVRT38479	11/75	Van	Southampton Publicity
9079	REL 743H	Bristol LH6L	LH300	10/69	Towing Vehicle	Grosvenor Square
9080	DCG 984S	Leyland Terrier	517695	8/77	Dropside Truck	CBW (Stores)
9081	OVX 685K	Ford Tractor Unit	51668	10/71	Recovery Crane	Salisbury (Trade Plates)
9082	Trade P	Atkinson Tanker	FC 9559	12/63	RecoveryVeh	Holdenhurst Rd B'mouth
9084	Trade Plates	AEC Matador	08538557	-/60	Recovery Crane	Grosvenor Square
9085	Trade Plates	Bedford 6 Ton	10667	-	Recovery Crane	Basingstoke
9086	OPN 801	Bristol LD5gB	138298	6/59	Tree Cutter	Poole
9087	NLJ 52EN	Bristol LH6L	LHB94	2/74	Recovery Vehicle	Poole
9088	REL 745H	Bristol LH6L	302	9/69	Towing Vehicle	CBW
9089	HCG 359N	Leyland Terrier	479943	4/75	Dropside Truck	CBW (Stores)

1 June 1981

Hants & Dorset Service Fleet, June 1981

Details of NBC service fleets are not often published. Fortunately the company included such vehicles in its official fleet list. Here is June 1981's service vehicles, including details and allocations.